*i*MARRIAGE
STUDY GUIDE

*i*MARRIAGE

STUDY GUIDE

ANDY STANLEY

Multnomah® Publishers *Sisters, Oregon*

iMARRIAGE STUDY GUIDE
published by Multnomah Publishers, Inc.

© 2006 by North Point Ministries, Inc.
International Standard Book Number: 1-59052-665-1

Cover Design by Andrew Cochran at Circle@Seven Studio

Unless otherwise indicated, Scripture quotations are from:
The Holy Bible, New International Version
© 1973, 1984 by International Bible Society,
used by permission of Zondervan Publishing House

Multnomah is a trademark of Multnomah Publishers, Inc.,
and is registered in the U.S. Patent and Trademark Office.
The colophon is a trademark of Multnomah Publishers, Inc.

Printed in the United States of America

For information:
MULTNOMAH PUBLISHERS, INC.
601 N. LARCH ST.
SISTERS, OREGON 97759

06 07 08 09 10—10 9 8 7 6 5 4 3 2

CONTENTS

Open Your "I"

by Andy Stanley

Once upon a time, you stood at the altar and began what you hoped would be a storybook marriage. Whether you realized it or not, it was a storybook you had written yourself. In fact, you had been writing it for years. Over a lifetime, you filled it with your dreams and desires, your pictures and plans of what you thought the ideal marriage would look like. *I dream of this…I long for that…*in essence, you started out with an *I*-marriage.

There's just one problem. Your spouse started out with an *I*-marriage too. And when two plots merge together in the same story…well, it's just a matter of time before somebody gets their *I* crossed. Often, the stronger spouse becomes the primary author of the marriage, while the other lives in quiet frustration. Or perhaps the two will agree to compromise, taking turns writing a chapter, but never fully realizing their version of what they'd dreamed. Sadly, many couples conclude that their vision of *marriage* was really just a *mirage*. Over time, they settle into an unspoken arrangement that barely resembles the happy marriage they once imagined.

The good news is that God doesn't intend for us to abandon our heartfelt hopes and dreams. After all, He is the one who put those desires in us. But He has a different avenue of seeing those desires met than dumping them on our spouse. When we learn how to effectively handle our desires and expectations in marriage we're on the way to discovering a new kind of marriage that's more fulfilling than we ever imagined marriage could be.

Great Expectations

If we're honest, we'll admit that we all approach marriage with a set of desires and wishes that we hope will be realized as a result of forming a union with our spouse. We have ideas about when we'll have children, how we'll spend time together, and what lifestyle we'll enjoy.

But what happens when our dreams for marriage fail to materialize? What if your partner never gets around to doing his or her part so you can finally experience life as you've always envisioned it? What if your ideas for life as a married person collide with your partner's ideas? In this session, we'll look at four common responses when our box full of dreams gets shelved. And we'll discover the difference between pouring your heart and soul into a marriage and pouring it into the person you love.

MY BOX OF DREAMS

From early childhood, most people dream of getting married someday. We have vivid mental images of what it will
look like and feel like to finally be a married person. We
imagine where we'll live, what we'll drive, where we'll go on
vacation, and how many children we'll have. Many people
have detailed ideas of what they'll talk about, what they'll do
on Saturday afternoons, or what they'll eat on Wednesday
nights. What are some of the dreams of marriage you always
envisioned before you were married?

EXERCISE

VIDEO NOTES
(READ THIS OR WATCH SESSION 1 OF THE DVD)

We all approach marriage with a picture of how it is going to be. Even if you are single you have already begun to imagine what marriage should look like: She will submit. He will submit. We'll save money. We'll spend money. We will spend our discretionary time together. I need my space and friends. Christmas is just us in our own little bungalow. Christmas is at my mom's with all my aunts, uncles, and cousins…

At the center of all this is "I." I imagine. I desire. I have always thought. I expect. We have drawn a picture of marriage designed for me and by me. Bottom line, we have agendas for the people we are marrying. And wouldn't you know it, your spouse also has an agenda and a set of expectations as well. They have an "I."

Eventually the I's collide, and we all react in one of four ways:

The first option is to **leave**. "This is not what I thought it would be." The problem with this option is that we take "I" with us. We just move on and dump our expectations on someone else.

The second option is to **conquer** and try to change our spouses. This is an attempt to get "her" to be "I."

The third option is to **conform**. When we conform we try to become somebody we are not. "I won't be 'I,' I'll be 'him.'" On the surface things look good. But eventually, the truth surfaces and somebody is taken by complete surprise.

The fourth option is to **compromise**. This works great for a while. However, compromise is still about "I." "I will as long as you will." "Didn't we do it your way last time?" Compromise leads to scorekeeping and it kills intimacy. It is really another way to be committed to "I" because I want MY marriage to work out.

While there are areas in your marriage where compromise is important, at some point you should move beyond compromise as a way of dealing with your differences. We'll talk about the best way for handling differences over the next several sessions. In this session, we'll stop to identify how you have been handling your expectations thus far.

{ *" What a happy and holy fashion it is that those who love one another should rest on the same pillow. "* —*Nathaniel Hawthorne* }

[NOTES]

DISCUSSION QUESTIONS

Take a few moments to discuss your answers to these questions with the group.

1. How have the following affected your expectations going into marriage? What pictures of marriage have you tried to imitate or avoid?

   imitate ■ TV

   imitate ■ Books or magazines

   avoid ■ Your parents' marriage(s)

   both ■ Other marriages

2. Have you ever felt like you just couldn't measure up—that you just couldn't meet the expectations you felt were placed upon you? Maybe this occurred with your parents, your spouse, your boss, a coach, or someone else. How did this affect the relationship?

3. What about leaving? Why is this option sometimes tempting? What is the problem with this option?

4. Have you ever tried to make your spouse more like you? Does it work? What message does this give your spouse?

5. When expectations collide, one of the most popular options is to compromise. However, compromise can backfire when you are more committed to your marriage than your partner. Have you observed this?

MILEPOSTS

■ Everyone comes into marriage with a set of wishes and desires.

■ When our desires for marriage turn into expectations, conflict ensues.

■ Four common responses to conflict in marriage: we run, we conquer, we conform, we compromise.

WHAT WILL YOU DO?

This week, list two or three examples of the weight of expectations in your life.

THINK ABOUT IT

God doesn't call you to be committed to marriage; He calls you to be committed to your spouse. If you think about it, it's possible to give "honor" to marriage while unloading expectations on your spouse. So what about you? Where does your commitment lie?

CHANGING YOUR MIND

In the Bible, God gives us instructions for a successful marriage . Renew your mind by meditating on God's Word this week.

"Wives, in the same way be submissive to your husbands so that, if any of them do not believe the word, they may be won over without words by the behavior of their wives, when they see the purity and reverence of your lives."

1 Peter 3:1–2

DAILY DEVOTIONS

To help you prepare for session two, use these suggested devotions during the week leading up to your small group meeting.

DAY ONE

Read 1 Peter 2:21–3:1. What kind of example did Christ leave for us in how to love others? Today, focus on emulating Christ's example of unconditional love, even in the face of hostility.

DAY TWO

Read 1 Peter 3:1. In the same way that Christ expressed His love by submitting Himself, so wives are to express their love by submitting themselves to their husbands. How do expectations get in the way of fulfilling this command? As you go through the day, think about the expectations you place on your spouse.

Day Three

Read 1 Peter 3:1–2. When you submit to someone else, you gain favor in his or her eyes. How about when you place expectations on others? What kind of response does this elicit? Focus today on how people react to the weight of expectations that are placed on them.

Day Four

Read 1 Peter 3:7. In the same way that wives are to submit to their husbands, husbands are to be considerate and respectful toward their wives. One sign that we are placing expectations on our spouse is that we stop serving our spouse. As you go through the day, take note of how considerate you are of your spouse.

Day Five

Read 1 Peter 3:7 again. How does your relationship with your spouse impact your relationship with God? As you go through the day, pray that God would make you aware of the expectations you are placing on your spouse.

LAST WEEK...

We saw that conflicts in marriage result when our desires are allowed to turn into expectations. We also examined four common responses when our ideas for marriage remain unfulfilled: we run, we conquer, we conform, or we compromise.

When Expectations Collide

There's nothing wrong with having hopes and dreams for what your marriage will be like. But when those desires are allowed to harden into expectations, it changes the whole dynamic of the marriage. In fact, a marriage shaped by expectations more closely resembles a debt/debtor contract than a love relationship. The underlying message between the spouses is, "You owe me. And if you miss a payment, there could be severe penalties."

Not surprisingly, many couples learn to live with these trade-offs. Over the years, we get pretty good at recognizing what our counterpart expects, and we program ourselves to deliver. Likewise, we know when to push our spouses to get what we want.

But drifting into such an arrangement has devastating consequences. Because as we're about to see, negotiating around our expectations creates an environment devoid of the one thing we really need from marriage. And according to Scripture, it's the opposite of what God intended in the first place.

THAT WOULDN'T HAPPEN THERE

Match the following pieces of communication with the most appropriate description:

A letter from your credit card company.

A card from your fiancé.

A card from your spouse of ten years.

An e-mail from your boss.

- Gushing with adulation, sprinkled with perfume.
- Straight to the point, warning of consequences.
- Encouraging tone, obligatory in nature.
- Appreciative spirit, ulterior motives possible.

Can some descriptions be interchanged with others? Which ones? Why or why not?

VIDEO NOTES
(Read This or Watch Session 2 of the DVD)

Expectations over time will transform your marriage from a covenant relationship to a debt/debtor relationship. This is because of what expectations communicate: You owe me. Expectations reflect what you feel like you deserve. These may be very realistic expectations, but they ultimately lead to disappointment. I didn't get what I deserved. You didn't deliver what you owed me. Eventually you begin to move into a bargaining approach in order to manage expectations, but this impedes our ability to love. You see, an expectation is a request for something, while love is the gift of something. We end up in a tug-of-war that destroys intimacy and romance.

But the thing is, behind your and your spouse's expectations is a legitimate God-given desire. Everyone was born with desires. We desire to be cherished. We desire companionship. We desire acceptance. But when you take a legitimate desire and place it on the shoulders of your spouse it feels like an expectation. She owes me. And then when he gives you what you expect, are you grateful? Not at all! Wives are supposed to keep the house straight. Husbands are supposed to be the providers. It is this transfer that turns the covenant into a contract. There goes the love. Bring out the gloves.

So how do you keep good God-given desires from becoming harmful de-motivating expectations? How do you take an expectation and put it back into the category of a desire? How do I get "I" out of the middle of the relationship? You have to answer one foundational question. What does your spouse owe you? The answer to that question will pinpoint your expectations.

I think many of us walked up to the altar with desires and walked out the door of the church with expectations. To experience what God had in mind, you've got to take things out of the expectation box and put them back in the desire box. But watch out. The thing that will keep you from doing that is "I." *"I'm" afraid he/she will… "I" won't get what "I" need. "I" may not be happy.* If you can get beyond the "I" in marriage, you can move things out of the expectation box and back into the desire box.

> " *Success in marriage does not come merely through finding the right mate, but through being the right mate.* "
> —Barnett R. Brickner

[NOTES]

Its okay to desire things of
your spouse but its not okay to
expect things because if he meets
those expectations your just
getting up to "0" level

DISCUSSION QUESTIONS

Take a few moments to discuss your answers to these questions with the group.

1. Ingratitude is a symptom of shifting desires to expectations. You find yourself complaining about something not getting done, but rarely thanking your spouse when it does get done. Can you think of some examples of this in your marriage?

2. Another symptom is a lack of serving your spouse. You see something that needs to be done and do nothing about it because you expect your spouse to do it. Can you think of some examples of this in your marriage?

3. How do we justify our expectations?

4. When we turn desires into expectations, we begin to change our marriage from a covenant relationship to a contractual one. What is the difference between a covenant and a contract?

5. Expectations create a debt/debtor relationship in marriage. It becomes about what your spouse "owes" you. What do you feel that your spouse owes you?

6. How do expectations prevent unconditional love from being expressed?

MILEPOSTS

■ When our desires become expectations, "I love you" is replaced with "You owe me."

■ When expressions of love become debts owed rather than unconditional gifts, everything about marriage changes.

■ This change can rob the marriage relationship of the healthy elements of gratitude and service and replace them with criticism and selfishness.

WHAT WILL YOU DO?

This week, try to identify any debts you think your spouse "owes" you. Make a list. Have you believed you are owed certain experiences or opportunities…or to be treated a certain way? If you could change those expectations back to desires, how would it change the way you respond to your spouse? Would you express gratitude more often? Would you experience less frustration? What would it look like to convey unconditional love instead of your unspoken expectations?

THINK ABOUT IT

Now list two or three things you would owe God if He chose to take a debt/debtor approach with you. How has being free from obligation to God changed your life? How might being free from obligation in marriage affect your relationship with your spouse?

CHANGING YOUR MIND

As you meditate on this verse during the week, consider how you might apply it to your marriage. When you focus on what you can do for your spouse, you begin to take the "I" out of marriage.

"Husbands, in the same way be considerate as you live with your wives, and treat them with respect as the weaker partner and as heirs with you of the gracious gift of life, so that nothing will hinder your prayers."

1 PETER 3:7

DAILY DEVOTIONS

To help you prepare for session three, use these suggested devotions throughout the week leading up to your small group meeting.

DAY ONE

Read Ephesians 5:21. What does it look like to submit? As you go through the day, try to submit to others. Is this easy or hard?

DAY TWO

Read Ephesians 5:21 again. Great marriages are built around mutual submission. Why is it important for both spouses to submit in order for a marriage to work as God intended? As you go through the day, carry with you the picture of how your marriage would be different if both you and your spouse submitted to one another.

DAY THREE

Read Ephesians 5:21 again. What should be our motivation for submitting to one another? Meditate today on what Christ has done for you (1 Peter 2:21–3:1) and how that impacts the way you relate to your spouse and others.

Day Four

Read Ephesians 5:22. What does it look like for a wife to submit to her husband as to the Lord? Wives, today focus on submitting to your husband as to the Lord.

Day Five

Read Ephesians 5:25. What does it look like for a husband to love his wife as Christ loved the church? Husbands, today focus on loving your wife as Christ loved the church.

LAST WEEK...

We saw that our expectations have the capacity to turn marriage into nothing more than a contract. Rather than being free to give unconditional love, we find ourselves saying, "You owe me." In this kind of relationship, neither of us ever measures up.

One to Another

Like it or not, marriages eventually experience a collision of interests. Whether it's an unspoken desire or a full-blown set of expectations, the bottom line is the same. You have your hopes and dreams, and your spouse has his or hers. It's just a matter of time before they compete against one another. And when they do, conventional wisdom says that we should be willing to yield to the other person's desires out of love for him or her.

But there's a problem with that approach. What happens if you don't feel a lot of love toward your spouse at the time? What if your spouse doesn't deserve it? Or what if you're so tired of giving in to him or her that you just can't yield any longer?

The key to a successful marriage is having enough love to carry you both through the times of conflicting interests. And in this session, we'll examine a passage of Scripture that reveals a secret source of unending love for any marriage. As we're about to see, it's not really a matter of putting your spouse first—or your spouse putting you first—but learning to put yet a third person first instead.

THAT CHANGES EVERYTHING

It's amazing how your attitude toward someone can change based on who they know. A nameless neighbor suddenly becomes noteworthy when you discover he's the brother of your favorite teacher growing up. That lady in front of you in the grocery line isn't such a slowpoke when you realize it's your boss's wife. Have you ever experienced a sudden change in your attitude toward someone because of their relationship to someone else? Share examples.

How does it impact your attitude toward marriage to recognize that your spouse is a child of God?

EXERCISE

VIDEO NOTES
(READ THIS OR WATCH SESSION 3 OF THE DVD)

The only way to get everything out of the expectation box and back into the desire box is to conclude that your spouse doesn't owe you anything and that you owe him or her everything. This is pretty much the essence of a Christian marriage—mutual submission for Christ's sake.

Read Ephesians 5:21. "Submit to one another out of reverence for Christ." Now what does it mean to submit? Submission is placing the needs, desires, and dreams of someone else ahead of "I."

And look at our motivation for submitting. It does not say "out of reverence for one another," but rather "out of reverence for Christ." We are to express our gratitude to God through our treatment of the person we married. Think about this for a minute. It is like us going up to God and saying, "God, how can I say thanks? You love me in spite of me. You forgave me. You've blessed me. Now what can I do for you?" And God responding, "Go do the same for your husband or wife, not for their sake, but for mine." Hearing this we might want to ask, "Are there any other options? What if I go 11 percent? How about a mission trip?" But God wants us to be the vessels through which He pours out His love on our spouses.

Paul goes on to flesh out this mutual submission for both men and women. "Wives, submit to your husbands as to the Lord" (v. 22). Put your husband first as you put the Lord first. Place your husband's needs, wishes, and dreams ahead of yours. And ladies, you may push back because he doesn't deserve it. But that's just the point! He doesn't deserve it. Like you didn't. And for the men, "Husbands, love your wives, just as Christ loved the church and gave himself up for her" (v. 25). Men, lay down your life for your wife just like Christ laid down his life for you. Our wives should feel as if we would lay down our lives in order to protect them emotionally, physically, and financially. But she doesn't deserve it. That's the point.

{ *" We have the greatest pre-nuptial agreement in the world. It's called love. "*
—Gene Perret }

[NOTES]

_____
_____
_____
_____
_____
_____
_____
_____
_____
_____
_____
_____
_____
_____
_____
_____
_____
_____
_____
_____
_____

DISCUSSION QUESTIONS

Take a few moments to discuss your answers to these questions with the group.

1. What are the benefits of understanding God's instructions for marriage?

2. Read Ephesians 5:21. What does it mean to "submit to one another"? What keeps us from submitting to one another?

3. How does our culture view submitting to someone else?

4. What should be our motivation for submitting to one another? How does this make it easier to submit?

5. What does it look like for a wife to submit to her husband as to the Lord?

6. What does it look like for a husband to love his wife as Christ loved the church?

MILEPOSTS

- God desires that you show your gratitude to Him by showering love on our spouse.

- Submission to each other is not required because you deserve it, but because of what Christ has done for you.

- You are to love like He loves you.

WHAT WILL YOU DO?

This week, pay special attention to the times when your desires collide with your spouse's and you are forced to choose between big "I" and little "i." Keep a private list of these opportunities to "submit" to your spouse. Are there certain situations where patterns emerge? Do they point to any character issues in you?

THINK ABOUT IT

If God's goal is to conform you to Christ's likeness, why might God be allowing you to experience a collision of wills with your spouse? In the space below, list any character traits that God might be trying to refine in you. How would your character be transformed if you practiced deliberate submission and allowed God to soften your will in this area?

CHANGING YOUR MIND

Place this week's verse near a doorway in your home as a reminder to say "after you" to your spouse as an expression of love. Also, be reminded to stop daily to stand in utter awe of God and what He has done in Christ.

"Submit to one another out of reverence for Christ."

EPHESIANS 5:21

DAILY DEVOTIONS

To help you prepare for session four, use these suggested devotions throughout the week leading up to your group meeting.

DAY ONE

Read Ephesians 5:21–27. As Paul discusses marriage he continues to point to the relationship between Christ and the church. What are the things that Paul points out that Christ has done for His bride? Meditate today on Christ's love for the church.

DAY TWO

Read Ephesians 5:28–32. The unity inherent in marriage is an incredible analogy of Christ's relationship with the church. How does knowing this change your understanding of what marriage is all about? Focus today on how your love for your spouse models the relationship between Christ and the church.

DAY THREE

Read Ephesians 5:33. We are called to love our spouses, and when we do we tangibly express God's love for them. How does it make you feel to know that God has designated you as an instrument to reflect His love for your spouse? As you go through the day, take stock of how loved your spouse feels.

DAY FOUR

Read Ephesians 5:33 again. There are no conditions on this statement. It does not read, "if your spouse makes spending time with you a priority, then respect him." It does not read, "if your spouse puts your needs above hers, love her." Try to love your spouse today with no strings attached.

DAY FIVE

Read Ephesians 5:21–33. Submitting and loving your spouse with no strings attached is a scary thing. "But he'll take advantage of me." Focus on Christ's unconditional, no-strings-attached love and take the risk.

LAST WEEK...

We discovered that submitting to one another in love is the key to a successful marriage. Here's the twist: Our submission is to be motivated not by what our spouses deserve, but by our gratitude to Christ for what He has done.

Husbands and Wives

As we've seen so far, the key to marriage is keeping your desires from turning into expectations. But that's a lot easier said than done. After all, we're talking about your lifelong hopes and dreams. The stakes are high. How can you hope for something so important without going so far as to demand it? Besides, it's not like the things you want are unreasonable. Is it too much to ask that you get a little cooperation from your spouse along the way?

But as with many things in life, we learn that ultimate fulfillment doesn't come from realizing our personal hopes and dreams after all. Instead, ultimate satisfaction comes when we fulfill the role God created us to play in the universe. And marriage is no exception.

In this session, we'll see that marriage represents much more than just a personal box of hopes and dreams to be opened and experienced. It is a special assignment created by God uniquely for you. No one else can fulfill it. And if we're willing, we have the opportunity to experience something the Bible calls a mystery. All we have to do is exchange our purpose for marriage with God's purpose for marriage.

THE HIDDEN MEANING

If you look for it, there is often hidden meaning in many of our "routine" experiences in life. A meticulous janitor thinks he's simply doing his job, not realizing that his faithfulness is being noticed by hundreds of business people who need encouragement to face one more day. A thoughtful comment from a fellow church member happens to be just the affirmation you need to step out in faith on something you've been considering. What are some examples of "routine" encounters that have had a deep impact on your life?

We get married for lots of "surface" reasons. What are some of the purposes God might be pursuing below the surface?

EXERCISE

VIDEO NOTES
(READ THIS OR WATCH SESSION 4 OF THE DVD)

You have been chosen as God's number one method of expressing His love for your spouse.

So how do you do this? You can't unconditionally love your spouse until you get your expectations back in the proper box. And the only way to do that is to decide that your spouse doesn't owe you anything. Only then are you free to love. And only then can you experience the unconditional love of your spouse.

Now you may have hesitations. You fear what would happen if you put everything back in this box and just gave and gave and gave. "She will just take advantage of that." "He will abuse it." And if that is the way you think then you probably also believe that the only reason your spouse is behaving now is because of your expectations, your reminders, your notes, or your late-night conversations. Unfortunately, that's not called marriage. That's called parenting. If you take the pressure off, there's no telling what will happen.

What you need more than anything else in the world is what your spouse cannot give you as long as you insist on prodding and nagging and reminding and tugging. You need to experience unconditional—ungoaded love. That requires space. That requires the opportunity to give before being reminded. If you came out of a difficult family situation, you will always have a tendency to place on your spouse the expectations that were not met in your family of origin. And once you do that, he or she will live with the burden of pleasing someone that can't be pleased. And you will never feel loved because you have removed the margin necessary to love. And what you fear will become a reality— you will become disappointed in your marriage.

{ *"What counts in making a happy marriage is not so much how compatible you are, but how you deal with incompatibility."* *}*
— *George Levinger*

[NOTES]

DISCUSSION QUESTIONS

Take a few moments to discuss your answers to these questions with the group.

1. God designed marriage so that He could tangibly express His love for you. How does this truth change your understanding of marriage?

2. How does it make you feel to know that God has designated you as the primary instrument to reflect His love for your spouse?

3. In what ways are you guilty of parenting your spouse by trying to manage his or her behavior?

4. What are the fears associated with freeing your spouse from his or her "obligations" to you and deciding that your spouse doesn't owe you anything?

5. What are the benefits of freeing your spouse from your expectations?

6. If you were to decide that your spouse doesn't owe you anything, how would it change your interactions with him or her this week?

MILEPOSTS

■ God has given us to each other as His primary way to express His love in a tangible way.

■ You will never experience all that God has designed for your marriage if you act as a parent to your spouse.

■ By letting go of your expectations, while there are no guarantees, you open the door to hope for unconditional love in your marriage.

WHAT WILL YOU DO?

If you were given one chance to describe the character of Jesus Christ to your spouse, what are some of the words you would use? This week, write down the five most important characteristics of the person of Jesus Christ that you would want your spouse to fully realize in his or her life. You may use words like those describing the fruit of the Spirit (love, joy, peace…).

THINK ABOUT IT

God has called you to be a living, tangible picture of Christ to your spouse. How have you been doing? How does your example compare to the list of characteristics you made to describe Christ? Can you pick one word from the list to begin working on this week?

CHANGING YOUR MIND

It is very easy to get off of the love track. Our expectations, judgments, and selfishness threaten every day to derail us. Use this week's verse to keep your focus on the message God has given you to pass on to your spouse: His love.

"Wives, submit to your husbands as to the Lord...Husbands, love your wives, just as Christ loved the church and gave himself up for her."

EPHESIANS 5:22–25

DAILY DEVOTIONS

To help you prepare for session five, use these suggested devotions throughout the week leading up to your group meeting.

Day One

Read 1 Peter 5:5. God opposes (resists) the proud, those who think they can do life all on their own. How do you react to those around you who are prideful? As you go through the day, take note of when you become prideful.

Day Two

Read 1 Peter 5:5. God gives grace to the humble. In this context grace refers to what you need in the moment for the moment. When have you experienced grace like this? As you go through the day, take note of situations where you could be more humble.

Day Three

Read 1 Peter 5:6. "Humble yourself under God's mighty hand" is Old Testament language for declaring your dependency on God. How easy is it for you to say, "God, I need You!"? Today, practice humbling yourself before God.

Day Four

Read 1 Peter 5:7. Literally, we are given permission to unload on God. When is the last time you went to God with your anxiety/cares/concerns/fears/needs? Today, talk to God and be specific about what is on your mind.

Day Five

Read 1 Peter 5:7 again. He cares for you. Think about that. Do you feel like God is concerned about you? Meditate today on the fact that you matter to God.

LAST WEEK...

We saw that a marriage where expectations rule is like parenting. We began to see that God has much, much more in store for us if we will let go of our expectations and choose to love as He loves us.

It Takes Three

The Golden Rule is widely accepted as a good principle for relationships. When we treat other people right, there's a better
chance that they'll treat us right in return. It's only logical. And when
you examine the Bible's instructions for marriage, there's a tendency to
think it's nothing more than another way of restating the Golden Rule.
After all, we should love our spouse the way we want to be loved. And
the unstated assumption is that we'll end up being treated better ourselves.

But God's involvement in marriage goes far beyond simply leaving
us an explanation of how relationship dynamics work, or teaching us
how to behave. God is a real person who interacts in our lives—and our
marriages—in real time.

In this session, we'll examine Scripture that makes two audacious
promises about God's involvement in your marriage. And suffice it to
say, it can either work for you or against you. It's confirmation that God
is active and involved in your personal circumstances. And He's
intensely interested in the outcome.

I CAN'T DO IT!

In the party game called "I Feel Deprived," each guest lists something he or she has never done. For example, you may say, "I have never gone hiking," or "I have never been to a zoo." If you are the only one who has been deprived of a particular experience, you win a point. Instead of sharing something with the group that you have not experienced, share something that you cannot do. For instance, "I can't whistle," or "I can't water ski." Try to think of something you're pretty sure everyone else can do. How does it feel to admit you can't?

How does this exercise help you relate to the fact that you just can't love your spouse without a lot of outside help from God?

E X E R C I S E

VIDEO NOTES
(READ THIS OR WATCH SESSION 5 OF THE DVD)

Once you have dumped everything from the expectation box back into the desire box, what's next? You've still got all these desires, hopes, and dreams. What are you supposed to do with them?

Let's look at a passage that answers that question, 1 Peter 5:5–7.

> "Young men, in the same way be submissive to those who are older. All of you, clothe yourselves with humility toward one another, because, 'God opposes the proud but gives grace to the humble.' Humble yourselves, therefore, under God's mighty hand, that he may lift you up in due time. Cast all your anxiety on him because he cares for you."

Peter begins with the general truth that God opposes (resists) the proud...just like we do. But He gives grace to the humble. What an extraordinary promise! In this context we can think of grace in this way: He gives you what you need in the moment for the moment. He doesn't make unreasonable demands of us. He gives us the ability to do what we need to do. Then Peter follows this up with a general command to humble yourself under God's mighty hand. This is Old Testament language for declaring your dependency on God. Peter is saying, "Tell God you need Him!" But doesn't this make perfect sense? Who designed you with those desires? Who understands them best? Who knows best how to meet them? And thus whom should we take them to?

Cast your cares (anxieties/concerns/fears/needs) on Him. God is giving us permission here. "Unload on me! Talk to me and be specific. No need to be polite. Vent. Dump." Why? He cares for you. Your desires and dreams matter to Him even if they don't seem to matter to your partner right now. And in response, you will find the grace to carry on. We've already talked about what happens when you dump your expectations on your spouse. He or she simply wasn't designed to handle them. But we have a heavenly Father who can handle them. So, cast your cares on Him.

{
" Marriage is a feast where the grace is
sometimes better than the dinner. "
—*Charles Caleb Colton*
}

[NOTES]

DISCUSSION QUESTIONS

Take a few moments to discuss your answers to these questions with the group.

1. God opposes the proud by withdrawing His help. Why does God do this? Have you ever felt that you were struggling without God's help because of pride?

2. Grace in this passage refers to the power to do what you need in the moment, for the moment. Have you ever felt this when you humbly asked for God's help?

3. "In due time" doesn't usually mean immediately. Why would God wait to meet your desires? When have you experienced this kind of waiting period?

4. Why do we tend to dump our desires on our spouses and not on God? Which of the two is best able to meet our desires?

5. What are ways that you can cast your cares upon God?

6. How does it make you feel to know that God is concerned about you and your desires? How would you approach God differently if you took this to heart?

MILEPOSTS

- God opposes the proud and gives grace to the humble.

- His grace means the power to do what is needed at the moment.

- If you will humble yourself, He will intervene on your behalf.

- Although He may not intervene immediately, you can express all your desires to Him as you wait.

WHAT WILL YOU DO?

This may take some time. Go to God in prayer—either silently, aloud, or on paper—and do what I Peter 5:7 says: cast your anxieties and cares on Him. You may need to express them in detail in order to fully roll them out to Him. You may need to stop and remember that even those desires that seem insignificant to you are important to God because you are important to Him.

THINK ABOUT IT

The idea of loving your spouse unconditionally can be terrifying. What if he or she takes advantage of you? If that's how you feel, it could be that you've never fully trusted God as the One who can look out for your needs. Casting your cares on God is an ongoing exercise. Practice it this week.

CHANGING YOUR MIND

Perhaps of all God's commands, the one to humble yourself bears the most repeating.

Pride can be pretty persistent. Ask God to use His Word this week to put you on the road to true humility.

"Humble yourselves, therefore, under God's mighty hand, that he may lift you up in due time. Cast all your anxiety on him because he cares for you."

I Peter 5:6–7

DAILY DEVOTIONS

To help you prepare for session six, use these suggested devotions throughout the week leading up to your small group meeting.

DAY ONE

Read Genesis 2:18. In the beginning God created the first "us." He knew that it was not good for Adam to live in lonely isolation, so He created Eve. Today, think about how expectations drive "us" apart.

DAY TWO

Read Genesis 2:19–22. In this context the word "helper" is probably best understood as "companion." Adam and Eve were complements, each supplying what the other was lacking. Celebrate today the desires that have been fulfilled by your companion.

DAY THREE

Read Genesis 2:23. Eve was created out of Adam. They were literally one flesh, the picture of unity. How can open communication keep a married couple united? Think today about anything that you have been holding back that you need to share with your spouse.

DAY FOUR

Read Genesis 2:24. When a man and woman come together in marriage, they are coming from two different families with two different personalities and carrying two sets of expectations. The two "I"s collide and somehow they become one. As we come to the end of this study, are there still any lingering expectations that you are holding on to? Today, work on identifying any such expectations.

DAY FIVE

Read Genesis 2:25. In the beginning, there was no shame. The intimacy that Adam and Eve shared was untainted. Today, focus on being vulnerable and transparent with your spouse as you work on regaining intimacy in your marriage. Then your marriage can be what God intended it to be when He put the first woman and the first man together.

LAST WEEK...

We discovered the reason so many marriages don't work: Pride. If we can learn to humble ourselves and place our concerns beneath the concerns of our spouse, we will experience God's aid and intervention.

Box Talk

As a husband or a wife, you can learn everything there is to know about how relationships work and how God designed marriage. Likewise, your spouse can do the same. But sooner or later, the success of your marriage hinges on the quality and effectiveness of your communication as you work through the details of life together. If communication is clear and honoring, and if there's plenty of it, then both parties gain a tremendous ability to understand and appreciate each other. They can learn how to anticipate each other's needs, and they tend to place sincere value on their spouse's desires.

But communication isn't easily mastered. Sure, it comes easy for some. But for others it can be an ongoing struggle. Depending on your upbringing, it may be completely unnatural to have an intentional conversation about how you feel, or how to improve your relationship.

That's why this session is dedicated to giving you a guide for talking to your spouse about your box of hopes and dreams—your desires. Following these three simple steps, you and your spouse can take a giant step toward a deeper understanding of each other—and how to keep unmet expectations from poisoning your marriage.

ARE YOU LISTENING?

There's a fine line between conversation and monologue. What we call conversation is often nothing more than two people taking turns unloading their thoughts in alternating monologues. But real conversation requires that we develop the art of listening to the other person. To set the tone for this session, show that you've been listening by sharing one thing with the group that you've heard your spouse say in the past week.

EXERCISE

VIDEO NOTES

(READ THIS OR WATCH SESSION 6 OF THE DVD)

After you have cast your cares on God and you are ready to talk with your spouse about what's in the box, here are some practical tips on how to have that conversation:

First you need to **Confess**. Take responsibility for turning your desires into expectations. And make sure you are specific, whether it is the expectation to make more money, keep the house cleaner, be more organized, be in better shape, or spend more time with the kids. Confess your expectations.

Then **Ask**. Ask the questions: "Where do you feel pressure to live up to my expectations?" "What can I do to make our marriage richer?" Then don't say anything. Just listen. This is just another way of asking, "What's in your box?" But don't ask that. Now, when you are asked this, there may be some things in your desire box that don't need to come out. There are some things that need to stay between you and God. For example, don't share this with your spouse, "I've always dreamed of being married to a man who had made his fortune by forty and could retire and we could just travel together and live at the beach." You need to keep that in the box. Cast that on the Lord. That's a dream you are likely going to have to die to.

Now, the last step is to **Reward**. Reward your spouse like you did when you were dating. You see, the problem with expectations is that we don't reward people who meet them. "That's their job." "She's supposed to cart the kids around." "He is supposed to mow the grass." So when your spouse gets it right, reward that. Because what's rewarded gets repeated. One specific way to reward is to write thank-you notes and be specific in your gratitude. Sometimes we don't know what is a big deal until someone tells us.

When God created Adam and Eve and put them into the garden, He created the first "us." Not two "I's," but one "us." And that is God's desire for your marriage. And that doesn't happen until you transfer your expectations back into the desire box and you learn to unconditionally love each other.

> " *He felt now that he was not simply close to her, but that he did not know where he ended and she began.* "
> —Leo Tolstoy

[NOTES]

DISCUSSION QUESTIONS

Take a few moments to discuss your answers to these questions with the group.

1. What is the difference between talking to your spouse about your desires and talking to your spouse about your expectations?

2. What are some desires that your spouse has fulfilled for you?

3. How can you creatively find out what is in your spouse's desire box without directly asking him or her?

4. What are the dangers of unloading all of your unfulfilled desires on your spouse?

5. What are some ways that you can reward your spouse?

6. Where, when, and how will you have your first Box Talk?

MILEPOSTS

Use this helpful acronym to guide you in your "Box Talk":

- **Confess** first.

- **Ask** these two questions: "Where do you feel pressure to live up to my expectations?" and "What can I do to make our marriage richer?"

- **Reward** your spouse with gratitude when he or she meets one of your specific desires.

WHAT WILL YOU DO?

This week, decide where, when, and how you will have your first Box Talk. Document your intentions by writing those plans in the space below.

THINK ABOUT IT

The Box Talk doesn't always have to be a formal conference. In fact, as it becomes a part of your ongoing routine, it should find its way into everyday conversation. Make it a goal with your spouse to speak openly about each others' desires. The more you practice healthy communication, the easier it will be to recognize and meet each others' needs.

CHANGING YOUR MIND

Use this week's verse to remind you to take the "I" out of your marriage. Commit to unconditionally love her. Commit to unconditionally respect him.

"However, each one of you also must love his wife as he loves himself, and the wife must respect her husband."

EPHESIANS 5:33

Leader's Guide

So, You're the Leader...

Is that intimidating? Perhaps exciting? No doubt you have some mental pictures of what it will look like, what you will say, and how it will go. Before you get too far into the planning process, there are some things you should know about leading a small-group discussion. We've compiled some tried and true techniques here to help you.

BASICS ABOUT LEADING

1. **Don't teach…facilitate**—Perhaps you've been in a Sunday school class or Bible study in which the leader could answer any question and always had something interesting to say. It's easy to think you need to be like that too. Relax. You don't. Leading a small group is quite different. Instead of being the featured act at the party, think of yourself as the host or hostess behind the scenes. Your

primary job is to create an environment where people feel comfortable and to keep the meeting generally on track. Your party is most successful when your guests do most of the talking.

2. **Cultivate discussion**—It's also easy to think that the meeting lives or dies by *your* ideas. In reality, what makes a small-group meeting successful are the ideas of everyone in the group. The most valuable thing you can do is to get people to share their thoughts. That's how the relationships in your group will grow and thrive. Here's a rule: The impact of your study material will typically never exceed the impact of the relationships through which it was studied. The more meaningful the relationships, the more meaningful the study. In a sterile environment, even the best material is suppressed.

3. **Point to the material**—A good host or hostess gets the party going by offering delectable hors d'oeuvres and beverages. You too should be ready to serve up "delicacies" from the material. Sometimes you will simply read the discussion

questions and invite everyone to respond. At other times, you may encourage someone to share his own ideas. Remember, some of the best treats are the ones your guests will bring to the party. Go with the flow of the meeting, and be ready to pop out of the kitchen as needed.

4. **Depart from the material**—A talented ministry team has carefully designed this study for your small group. But that doesn't mean you should follow every part word for word. Knowing how and when to depart from the material is a valuable art. Nobody knows more about your people than you do. The narratives, questions, and exercises are here to provide a framework for discovery. However, every group is motivated differently. Sometimes the best way to start a small-group discussion is simply to ask, "Does anyone have a personal insight or revelation he'd like to share from this week's material?" Then sit back and listen.

5. **Stay on track**—Conversation is the currency of a small-group discussion. The more interchange, the healthier the "economy." However, you need to keep your objectives in

mind. If your goal is to have a meaningful experience with this material, then you should make sure the discussion is contributing to that end. It's easy to get off on a tangent. Be prepared to interject politely and refocus the group. You may need to say something like, "Excuse me, we're obviously all interested in this subject; however, I just want to make sure we cover all the material for this week."

6. **Above all, pray**—The best communicators are the ones who manage to get out of God's way enough to let Him communicate *through* them. That's important to keep in mind. Books don't teach God's Word; neither do sermons or group discussions. God Himself speaks into the hearts of men and women, and prayer is our vital channel to communicate directly with Him. Cover your efforts in prayer. You don't just want God present at your meeting, you want Him to direct it.

We hope you find these suggestions helpful. And we hope you enjoy leading this study. You will find additional guides and suggestions for each session in the Leader's Guide notes that follow.

Leader's Guide
Session Notes

SESSION 1—GREAT EXPECTATIONS

KEY POINT

Unless the couples in your group have been married a very, very short time, today's topic will resonate deeply with them. All of us have dreams and desires, and marriage is probably the most fertile ground for those dreams to grow. It is also the easiest place for disappointment to develop. In many ways, this first session is opening another box. As the couples in your group begin to identify their desires, they are opening the box of growth and change.

EXERCISE—MY BOX OF DREAMS

The purpose of this exercise is to get the group thinking about their own desires. Keep the discussion light and fun. Every person in the group had a picture of what marriage would be like before they were married. Encourage honesty, but steer away from allowing one spouse to "dump" his or her disappointments on the group.

NOTES FOR DISCUSSION QUESTIONS

1. How have the following affected your expectations going into marriage? What pictures of marriage have you tried to imitate or avoid?

   - TV
   - Books or magazines
   - Your parents' marriage(s)
   - Other marriages

   Our culture loudly asserts its views on us every day. Once the discussion gets started, there is a lot to say about this. Talk about how idealistic and skewed the perspective is that is offered by many of these influences.

2. Have you ever felt like you just couldn't measure up—that you just couldn't meet the expectations you felt were placed upon you? Maybe this occurred with your parents, your spouse, your boss, a coach, or someone else. How did this affect the relationship?

   Our real selves are lost in relationships where we are trying to reach a certain standard in order to gain the approval of others. The people-pleasers in the group may take comfort in hearing from each other. Because they are typically less quick to express their opinions in a group, give them adequate time to answer.

3. What about leaving? Why is this option sometimes tempting? What is the problem with this option?

   Leaving is the easy way out. Sealing off the exit in marriage means both spouses are able to learn and grow. When a husband or wife leaves a marriage, at least half of the problem leaves. This question can provide a time to offer hope.

4. Have you ever tried to make your spouse more like you? Does it work? What message does this give your spouse?

   It may be easier to discuss relationships other than marriage when answering this question, if it is obvious this is an issue for the couples present. Discuss the tragedy of a relationship that is consistently on a lose/win basis.

5. When expectations collide, one of the most popular options is to compromise. However, compromise can backfire when you are more committed to your marriage than your partner. Have you observed this?

   Discuss the problems with a 50/50 marriage. This is a setup for continual conflict, as each partner pushes and pulls for his or her per-centage. Has anyone tried this, only to discover it doesn't work? Why didn't it?

What Will You Do?

"Giving honor to marriage" goes far beyond refraining from adultery. This exercise is intended to get participants thinking about the true meaning of honor in day-to-day situations.

Think About It

As this segment suggests, if we focus on honoring our spouse, the health of the marriage seems to take care of itself. This may be a new realization for many people in your group. Many people revere the concept of marriage, yet overlook the call to revere their spouses.

Daily Devotions

Don't forget to point out that there are optional daily devotions that the members can complete for the next session. These devotions will enable them to dig into the Bible and to start wrestling with the topics that will come up next time.

SESSION 2—WHEN EXPECTATIONS COLLIDE

KEY POINT

When a marriage consists of two people dumping expectations on each other, it becomes a contractual relationship. The participants in your group may be shocked to think of their marriages as debt/debtor unions, but that thought may be just what is needed to move each person to the higher plan God has for them. As they realize the truth about what holding onto their expectations can do to their marriages, they will hopefully desire to pursue a marriage of unconditional love.

EXERCISE—THAT WOULDN'T HAPPEN HERE

This exercise is designed to highlight the contrast between all other relationships and the marriage relationship. It could be that there are those in your group who need to have marriage lifted back to its highest value in their minds.

Notes for Discussion Questions

1. Ingratitude is a symptom of shifting desires to expectations. You find yourself complaining about something not getting done, but rarely thanking your spouse when it does get done. Can you think of some examples of this in your marriage?

   Of course you can! It may be helpful for husbands and wives to see that the frustrations in their marriages are similar to everyone else's. Note the similarities in answers. The men will probably have answers that are a lot alike, and the women will also.

2. Another symptom is a lack of serving your spouse. You see something that needs to be done and do nothing about it is because you expect your spouse to do it. Can you think of some examples of this in your marriage?

   In busy households, especially where there are children, the workload is often more than two people can handle. It might be helpful to acknowledge that fact here. If a husband grew up in a home where the men did no housework, he may feel justified in not helping in this area. Similarly, if a wife grew up in a home where her mother never took care of the cars, she may expect her husband to take over in that area. Discuss the dangers of these role expectations.

3. How do we justify our expectations?
   Perhaps we feel overworked, underappreciated, even used. These feelings can lead to a feeling that what we want is justified. Discuss how powerful justifying our expectations can be.

4. When we turn desires into expectations, we begin to change our marriage from a covenant relationship to a contractual one. What is the difference between a covenant and a contract? In attempting to understand what a covenant is, look to the covenant relationship we have with God based on the work of Christ. Discuss how lost we would be if we had a contract relationship with God!

5. Expectations create a debt/debtor relationship
   in marriage. It becomes about what your
   spouse "owes" you. What do you feel that your
   spouse owes you?

   The feeling that someone is obligated to us
   can be a very powerful emotion. Discuss how
   this comes about in marriage. You may touch
   on this in a surface way: My husband owes
   me flowers on my birthday. My wife owes me
   a day of golf with her blessing. Or you may
   dig deeper.

6. How do expectations prevent unconditional
   love from being expressed?

   You may touch on the obvious fact that
   expectations *are* conditions, but try to take
   the group deeper by drawing them into a discussion of how we need to actively replace
   those conditions with acts of selfless love.

WHAT WILL YOU DO?

This exercise is the beginning. As couples identify areas where they have allowed their desires to become expectations, and their expectations have turned into debts, they can address them head-on and eradicate them. This may be a difficult exercise for some because they are wondering what to do with their strong desires. That will come. Simply identifying the unspoken desires of the heart can be a very helpful first step.

THINK ABOUT IT

This exercise helps to put our "demands" back into perspective. When participants revisit their own need for grace, it will help them feel the importance of extending it to others. Understanding this truth about our sin and God's forgiveness through Christ is the heart of the gospel. It is the foundation of every other relationship. You may ask if anyone in the group has understood this and accepted it for the first time.

DAILY DEVOTIONS

Don't forget to point out that there are optional daily devotions that the members can complete for the next session. These devotions will enable them to dig into the Bible and to start wrestling with the topics that will come up next time.

SESSION 3—ONE TO ANOTHER

KEY POINT

If compromise is not the answer, what is? There are two keys to expressing true love in marriage. First, submit to one another. It's easy to think we are to submit because of our love for our spouse, but that kind of submission just isn't enough. The second key unlocks the motivation for submission. We are to submit because of what Christ has done for us. It is only in awe and appreciation of Him that we can have the kind of love needed to make marriage work.

EXERCISE—THAT CHANGES EVERYTHING

This exercise introduces an important concept for this session. We often value people based on their connection to another person. In this session, we learn that God instructs us to value our spouse based on their relationship to Jesus Christ.

NOTES FOR DISCUSSION QUESTIONS

1. What are the benefits of understanding God's instructions for marriage?

   Most people know their marriages needs improvement. This question can spark a hopeful discussion about the potential for growth.

2. Read Ephesians 5:21. What does it mean to "submit to one another"? What keeps us from submitting to one another?

   Discuss any previously-held views of submission. Why is this such a difficult word for most of us? Submission needs to be understood in the correct sense.

3. How does our culture view submitting to someone else?

   There are some pretty drastic stereotypes of the submissive wife in most people's minds. Try to paint a picture of what submission looks like to the world.

4. What should be our motivation for submitting to one another? How does this make it easier to submit?

   Discuss the connection between our awe of Christ and our submission to each other. It may be there are those who can share an example of a time when they submitted or served purely out of obedience to the Lord and it led to a change of heart.

5. What does it look like for a wife to submit to her husband as to the Lord?

   Women only! Discuss your answers and then let the men respond to them.

6. What does it look like for a husband to love his wife as Christ loved the church?

   Men only! Discuss your answers and then let the women respond to them.

WHAT WILL YOU DO?

When you analyze it, our conflicts in marriage often revolve around recurring issues or themes. Taking the time to identify these issues can teach us a lot about ourselves and what God is trying to accomplish in us.

THINK ABOUT IT

The goal of this segment is to practice taking information about our conflicts and translating it into specific character qualities. It's hard to understand what happens in a conflict. But it's much easier to focus on a character issue God is working on. When we understand that God wants to refine our character, we can begin to work with Him on that effort.

DAILY DEVOTIONS

Don't forget to point out that there are optional daily devotions that the members can complete for the next session. These devotions will enable them to dig into the Bible and to start wrestling with the topics that will come up next time.

SESSION 4—HUSBANDS AND WIVES

KEY POINT

This week's message is about a calling that is both noble and daunting. To be God's primary messenger of His love to my spouse is a tall order indeed. It can also be a privilege that gives the task of relating in marriage new meaning. The group may turn a corner this week, not only in focusing on the mistake of turning expectations into desires, but also on the incredible task God has given each of us.

EXERCISE—THE HIDDEN MEANING

As is often the case in life, God is up to much more in our lives than we first realize. As we're about to learn, God wants more for us than simply having a great marriage—He wants to give us the higher purpose of revealing Himself to our spouse. This exercise sets the stage for the assignment we are told God has given us in our marriages. It is a phenomenal thought that God would use us to express His love most tangibly to our spouse, rather than some far away agent.

NOTES FOR DISCUSSION QUESTIONS

1. God designed marriage so that He could tangibly express His love for you. How does this truth change your understanding of marriage?

   This question may be a time of sharing "aha" moments. There may be those who, before now, have never viewed marriage this highly. It is the way God sees marriage.

2. How does it make you feel to know that God has designated you as the primary instrument to reflect His love for your spouse?

   You may want to give options: afraid, excited, privileged, nervous. Remember that these emotional reactions are not morally right or wrong. Encourage the participants of the group to embrace this new way of looking at marriage.

3. In what ways are you guilty of parenting your spouse by trying to manage his or her behavior?

   Be sure the members of the group do not answer for each other—a form of parenting in itself! It may be that the spouse with the strongest personality does this most. It may also be that the less assertive spouse is comfortable in the "child" role.

4. What are the fears associated with freeing your spouse from his or her "obligations" to you and deciding that your spouse doesn't owe you anything?

   These fears—that my spouse will never meet any of my desires—can be very strong. But it is necessary to face the fears before releasing my spouse from my expectations. It is important to know that there are no guarantees that we won't realize at least some of our fears.

5. What are the benefits of freeing your spouse from your expectations?

Talk about what it is like to get out of debt or to pay off a particularly onerous bill. The freedom a marriage can experience when expectations are gone is worth it.

6. If you were to decide that your spouse doesn't owe you anything, how would it change your interactions with him or her this week?

What would this new perspective free you to do, to serve, and to love? The answers to this question can, as the first question did, paint a picture of what awaits a marriage where neither spouse says, "You owe me."

WHAT WILL YOU DO?

The idea of being a picture of God can be hard to grasp. But when we break it down into specific attitudes, it's easier to relate. The purpose of this exercise is to help participants articulate what it means to be a picture of God to someone else.

THINK ABOUT IT

The next step is to take our understanding of what it means to be a picture of God and apply it to our own lives. This exercise helps the people in your group identify a specific attribute of Christ that they should begin developing. Pray that each person will truly listen and invite God to reveal His desires for transforming his or her character.

DAILY DEVOTIONS

Don't forget to point out that there are optional daily devotions that the members can complete for the next session. These devotions will enable them to dig into the Bible and to start wrestling with the topics that will come up next time.

SESSION 5—IT TAKES THREE

KEY POINT

If it hasn't come up yet, it will this week. What do we do with all those desires? If it isn't healthy or right to turn them into expectations, what do we turn them into? Surely God doesn't expect us to just swallow them, or deny them, or pretend they don't exist. Even those little wishes that whisper in our heads…what do we do with those? They don't just go away. This week's session provides the answer, a soul-satisfying answer to that question: God is a real person and is available to ensure that all of our true needs are always met.

EXERCISE—I CAN'T DO IT!

The first step towards dependence upon God is to admit the mess we've made of our independence. It is to admit that we can't do what He asks us to do. When it comes to loving as God wants us to love, the fact is we're sunk. This exercise is just a fun way to point out that fact.

NOTES FOR DISCUSSION QUESTIONS

1. God opposes the proud by withdrawing His help. Why does God do this? Have you ever felt that you were struggling without God's help because of pride?

   This may be uncomfortable for some members of the group to discuss. Pride is an ugly thing to admit, but we are all guilty of it. This may provide a turning point for some who have never connected God's help with our humility.

2. Grace in this passage refers to the power to do what you need in the moment, for the moment. Have you ever felt this when you humbly asked for God's help?

   We are often helped by the examples of how God worked in another's life. This can be a time of encouragement for others.

3. "In due time" doesn't usually mean immediately. Why would God wait to meet

your desires? When have you experienced this kind of waiting period?

Everyone knows what it's like to wait. Impatience with God is something almost everyone would admit to. It is what we do during this waiting time that determines much of who we become in the meantime.

4. Why do we tend to dump our desires on our spouses and not on God? Which of the two is best able to meet our desires?

Although the second question is rhetorical, it bears asking because we often—in the moment—forget that God is far more able to meet our needs than our spouse.

5. What are ways that you can cast your cares upon God?

Resist the temptation to turn this into a formula. One may journal their prayers, another may pray out loud. One may meet with God every morning, another every night. The main thing is that we do it.

6. How does it make you feel to know that God is concerned about you and your desires? How would you approach God differently if you took this to heart?

Often it is when we take everything to God—from the petty to the potent—that we get the perspective we need. Knowing that He cares for us individually makes us confident that He wants to hear from us.

WHAT WILL YOU DO?

There is tremendous benefit when we can finally identify the things that concern us. There is freedom when we can put our finger on what's troubling us. Laying our concerns before God ensures that we have successfully sorted out our desires.

THINK ABOUT IT

Fear can be a powerful inhibitor. The purpose of this segment is to further process our thoughts. In order to let go of our fear of having our needs neglected, we must thoroughly grasp God's promise to meet our needs and show His care for us.

DAILY DEVOTIONS

Don't forget to point out that there are optional daily devotions that the members can complete for the next session. These devotions will enable them to dig into the Bible and to start wrestling with the topics that will come up next time.

SESSION 6—BOX TALK

KEY POINT

One last question is probably surfacing in the minds of your group members. Okay, I am releasing my spouse of my expectations. I am communicating my desires to God. Does that mean I can't talk to my spouse about this? Submission doesn't mean lack of communication, but it does mean we should learn loving ways to communicate. This week's sessions highlights some very practical guidelines for talking to your spouse about your desires, because, yes, you can talk about them.

EXERCISE—ARE YOU LISTENING?

The bottom line in a healthy marriage relationship is truly listening to your spouse's concerns and becoming a student of his or her needs. If we're honest, most people really struggle to see beyond their own personal interests; we tend to view our spouses as just another person to meet our needs. This exercise forces us to produce evidence of our ability to listen; and it sets up the key concept of this session.

NOTES FOR DISCUSSION QUESTIONS

1. What is the difference between talking to your spouse about your desires and talking to your spouse about your expectations?

   By now, it should be apparent that what appears to be a subtle difference is, in reality, huge. The difference lies in the motivation, the tone, the placing of guilt or obligation.

2. What are some desires that your spouse has fulfilled for you?

   This can be a very healing time. There may be husbands or wives who never or rarely express appreciation for their spouse publicly. It can be music to someone's ears!

3. How can you creatively find out what is in your spouse's desire box without directly asking him or her?

   It is important in marriage to understand that the two of you are very different people and it would be a mistake to assume one knew what the other was thinking or needing.

4. What are the dangers of unloading all of your unfulfilled desires on your spouse?

You may ask if anyone has had a desire that changed drastically, or if anyone has had a totally unrealistic desire. (Not that they should share that desire!) It is all too easy to think good communication means we say everything.

5. What are some ways that you can reward your spouse?

This is a good time to listen. As others share what makes them feel valued, noticed, or appreciated, take note. Often, spouses don't know how to speak the language of gratitude in a way their husband or wife can understand.

6. Where, when, and how will you have your first Box Talk?

You may want to give couples a minute to put their heads together and set a date and time. This, in itself, can represent an expectation. Be careful to encourage couples to communicate about this.

WHAT WILL YOU DO?

The assignment described throughout this session is vital to the success of this series. This exercise is simply a stepping stone to ensure that each participant completes it.

THINK ABOUT IT

Another important concept is the idea that communication is not an event, but a process. This segment is intended to de-mystify the "Box Talk" and encourage each person to see it as something to be practiced ongoing.